Data
Entry
Excellence

Ivan B. Walters

Data
Entry
Excellence

Ivan B. Walters

Short

In conclusion, data entry stands as a cornerstone of modern business operations, facilitating the organization, accuracy, and accessibility of information critical for decision-making and efficiency. From transcribing handwritten documents to leveraging advanced software tools, data entry professionals play a pivotal role in maintaining data integrity and optimizing workflow. Through their attention to detail, proficiency in technology, and commitment to accuracy, they uphold standards that are essential for organizational success.

As industries continue to evolve and embrace digital transformation, the importance of data entry remains undiminished. The role of data entry professionals extends beyond mere clerical tasks, encompassing data quality management, compliance with regulations, and driving innovation through process optimization. By leveraging technology and implementing best practices, organizations can harness the full potential of their data assets, unlocking insights that drive informed decisions and sustainable growth.

In essence, data entry is not just about inputting data—it's about empowering organizations to harness the power of information to thrive in an increasingly complex and competitive landscape. As businesses continue to rely on data as a strategic asset, the role of data entry professionals will continue to be indispensable, ensuring that data remains accurate, reliable, and actionable. With a firm foundation in accuracy, efficiency, and integrity, data entry professionals are instrumental in shaping the future of business in the digital age.

Table of Contents

Work-from-Home Job: Clerical Data Entry

Y ou may make smart money while working at your own pace with clerical data entry jobs that you can do from the comfort of your own home. No commitment is necessary for either the part-time or full-time data entry jobs that are available to you. One of the most effective methods of earning money online these days is this:

You can't compare the data entry work to your average typing job. On the other hand, you won't have to interact with clients, make clients, make phone calls, etc., and the tasks are straightforward. To secure a job with most companies, you don't need any prior experience. You should be able to navigate a computer and the internet with a minimum level of understanding.

The clerical data entry position may call for prior experience at some firms. You also need to have a home computer with an internet connection. A clerical data entry job from home might be a good fit for you if you meet the requirements listed above. This position provides you with flexible part-time or full-time hours and an outstanding salary.

Clerical data input from home employment enables you to make $20 to $200 each day. All you need to do is email your resume to any of the trusted companies via the web. the web. You will receive step-by-step instructions that are straightforward to follow from the organization employing you. Since the training is supplied largely via the internet, you may join the data entry work at any of the firms around the globe, no matter where you are staying. Once you have acquired instructions from the organization, you need to start the work by inputting data online in the proper manner.

In order to start the clerical data input from home work, you may need a home office, even if the employer does not specify it. You require a home computer with a high-speed internet connection, an email account, familiarity with internet and browser usage, and some basic experience with Microsoft Office products.

If you wish to apply for the clerical data entry work-at-home job, then beware of scammers on the internet. There are certain firms that may require an upfront investment to acquire the job. Be wary of such firms. You should remember that you need not spend anything to acquire a data entry job.

Though home-based clerical data entry jobs allow regular individuals to make remarkable revenue online, there are hundreds of home data entry occupations that cost you money. In order to locate a credible organization providing clerical data entry jobs to work at home, you need to perform some inquiries. Or you may also seek the aid of specific websites that present a list of honest organizations providing home-based clerical data entry jobs.

Once you have enlisted with an honest firm, you might obtain regular money for your service. Most of the home data entry jobs are paid monthly, once or twice. These jobs are perfect for stay-at-home parents, housewives, handicapped people, college students, and retirees.

Since there is no pressure in clerical data entry jobs, you may work comfortably and make a smart income.

Running a Data Entry Business

Adata entry business (or should that be business) provides services like word processing, secretarial, transcription, and other typing projects. It is a legitimate way to earn a decent income using your home computer and your modest skills. If you want to start a data entry business, you need to consider the following points:

- ✓ Do you have the ability to evaluate the right opportunity?

- ✓ Can you understand what types of data entries are available and who your potential customers are?

- ✓ Do you know how to create a marketing database for your data entry business?

If your answer is yes to the above questions, you can consider starting a data entry business. If you want to succeed in this business, you need to develop a strong base of clients. As a business owner, you can acquire home-based data entry projects and clients from various sources, like local area businesses and individuals, independent contractor relationships, and online freelance networks.

If you are a home data entry business owner, then you can do data entry work for a data processing firm, or you can do transcription for a market survey company. You can get miscellaneous data entry projects. The quality and timely service would earn you a huge reputation and success.

The business to provide data entry services includes many projects like data entry for documents including directories, journal entries, market research, bill entries, registration forms, pay roll entries, and much more. You can select any one or more projects according to the abilities of your staff. The more you offer flexible, scalable, and sustainable service, the more you can earn.

Once you have gained a set of customers, you will start getting new ones from the references of the existing ones. Therefore, you can develop your business well. The data entry business flourishes well if you are willing to learn a new skill or software program.

A data entry business can help you earn a lot of money, and you can enjoy a wide variety of projects. If you have an excellent reputation and a classy database of past customers, you can earn more profits than you expected.

Since there are a number of data entry business opportunities available online, there are chances of scams. Some people fall victim to internet scams and lose their money and time. The main reason for losing money in a data entry business is an urgency-based emotional decision. However, deep knowledge and awareness about scam sites would help you avoid costly mistakes and earn profits.

There are various types of data entry services, like online data entry, offline data entry, offshore data entry, image data entry, and so on. Image data entry service includes data entry of scanned images, image capturing services, image clipping services and so on. It is a part of the data entry business, and you can provide this service to your clients if you can provide superior quality services and cost-effectiveness to them.

Like any other business, the business of data entry services requires error-free and timely work in order to achieve success. Since it is an ever-growing field, you can earn a permanent income from this business.

Data Entry Business: What's It All About?

A data-input company is one of the fastest-growing enterprises in the world. The data entry company is quick-paced, dynamic, and in continual motion. Therefore, in such a flexible environment, there is a necessity for ease of access to precise and complete information. Thus, it will be unsuitable whether you are a small firm or a major data entry organization, as information is a key asset in any situation.

In a data entry company, the more you have market analysis, specifics about your consumers, clients, and other significant aspects, the better you can gain from the market. With this precise style of business analysis, you may better understand your data-input company.

As today is the era of information, transforming data into information and distributing that information is highly vital in every corporate organization. There are constantly fresh issues and processes inherent in each commercial operation. These difficulties include new enterprises, mergers, and changes in technology, among others.

The accessibility, worth, and miscellany of information that any organization has at its disposal are gradually becoming more crucial for consumers. Thus, this is the primary key to the extent and prosperity of data-entry firms.

In any data entry business, most of the activities are document and image processing, mage enhancement, photo manipulation, catalog processing, data conversion, PDF document indexing, data entry from photos, online data capture, creation of new databases, data entry from hard or soft copy to any record layout, online order entry and tag-on, and insurance claim entry.

Then other service types include online indexed document repossession services, mailing lists, data cleansing, data warehousing and mining, audio transcriptions, tools and support, legal documents, indexing of documents and vouchers, online completion of services and responses to clients like in call centers, and the list goes on. This list of services is inexhaustible since there is so much information in every location, sector, and perception of the planet.

Data entry enterprises now have numerous elements and types. Different sorts of categories include data entry services, data input outsourcing, offshore data entry, data processing, online data services, copy-and-paste data entry services, web research data input, data conversion, form processing, and data entry reports. Then other components include catalog data entry, data entry for legal problems and papers, and many more, depending on the kind of field and information resource.

Then, aside from this, data publication is also quickly becoming a significant aspect of data input. This data publication service encompasses numerous features, including data enrichment, document management, web hosting, design and presentation, search engine optimization, making and publishing e-books, and producing data in several different forms.

For these vivid data operations, specialist data input software is devised. These data entry programs receive data from any method of input and store it on computers for future processing. The storage of all the data is termed a database. The data entry software makes linkages between the database and its application and continually checks for any potential input errors or mistakes.

Therefore, data entry enterprises are largely dependent on data entry software and other technologies used for data entry and processing. It's also the backbone of support for numerous firms and organizations.

Data Entry Services

In the quickly expanding business world, every firm, irrespective of size, has to manage massive amounts of complicated data in a cost-efficient manner. The firms need to manage databases for customers, invoicing, pay rolls, and so on. This rising demand for managing enormous databases requires imaginative data entry firms that can deliver useful data input services at a modest cost.

Using data entry firms will assist other organizations not only in minimizing time-consuming jobs but also in allocating their resources to develop the company.

If any of the firms suffer from manpower scarcity or need to spend more time on other strategic tasks, outsourcing the data entry projects to one of the top data entry businesses will help move the business to the next level. These organizations have experienced and qualified staff who can accomplish the data entry work properly.

The staff in data entry firms typically have particular abilities in MS Word, MS Excel, and other programs, and thus they provide support for processing bills, pay rolls, surveys, medical billing information, and much more. These firms have significant flexibility to satisfy the needs of their client companies. The customers need to supply any document, and the expert data entry operators at the company insert that information into the applicable computer application.

The data entry firms provide high-quality services, and they also provide timely delivery of data input jobs. They provide thorough and precise data entry services to client organizations, wherever they are on the globe. This is feasible because of the introduction of the internet, and consequently, online data entry firms are increasingly prevalent today.

While selecting a data entry firm, the other companies should assess the dependability of that company. There are several data entry firms that offer data input services by employing a double-keying procedure to assure correctness. The double-keying procedure entails re-keying the data into distinct files, which are then compared electronically with each other to deliver the correct results to the client organizations.

There are various adaptable data entry businesses that can aid in finishing the client company's data input tasks, irrespective of language or kind. Versatility in handling data entry tasks is one of the key reasons for outsourcing the projects to data entry firms.

The firms may also acquire their final product in any convenient way, such as through the internet, CD-R, CD-RW, etc. Generally, data entry firms give the final data entry output in a readily comprehensible style so that the client organizations may be freed of the load of data entry activities.

Choosing a trustworthy data entry company is still a time-consuming procedure. However, the effort would yield greater rewards. These organizations provide excellent data entry, data processing, and other related services and provide a solution to all information processing demands. Therefore, the client organizations may concentrate their effort and time on other company growth responsibilities.

Outsourcing data entry jobs to data entry firms not only saves time and effort but also money. These firms provide excellent-quality services that are cost-efficient too.

Data Entry from Home: Is It For You?

If you are seeking a respectable home-based career, data input from home is the finest alternative. Anyone who has basic computer knowledge and the capacity to access the internet may start working home-based data entry jobs. It is a work without any responsibility. You may work at your own leisure.

Data entry jobs provide flexible part-time or full-time schedules as well. You need not make any initial investment or pay beginning costs to acquire this job. It is a work-from-home job that gives amazing remuneration for your service.

Data input from home work does not demand any additional certification or expertise. However, some organizations may demand prior experience. But most of the organizations do not demand experience, and they even give training to the home-based workers. You may obtain either face-to-face or online training and can start the job comfortably from home. Since there is no pressure in this profession, stay-at-home parents, retirees, and college students may attempt to gain employment.

Data entry services include word processing and generic transcribing. You may start working on these sorts of tasks from home if you have solid expertise in grammar, adequate typing speed, and accuracy. The ability to follow directions supplied by the organization employing you is a crucial attribute. You may obtain high remuneration for data input from home employment. Most of the firms deliver the payment monthly, once or twice, in the form of checks.

Due to swift advances in the world of business, both small and major firms find it challenging to manage massive amounts of complicated data. Hence, they outsource the data entry and processing duties to other organizations. These organizations choose home-based data entry operators like you to execute the duties. Since most firms are in huge need of data processing support, the data input from a home job might provide steady income.

There are various online data entry organizations that provide home-based data entry jobs. However, there may be a potential for fraud. If any firm demands registration money or training expenses, be wary of such a company. Generally, most respectable organizations do not charge anything for home-based data input workers.

You may also evaluate honest firms by putting their names in the search box of the Better Business Bureau. If any business claims to make you wealthy overnight or if any organization emphasizes that you can work for an hour and earn $1000 or more each day, then beware of such firms. No one can get wealthy without work.

Like any other profession, data input from home also demands some talent and effort. However, you may enjoy the ease of working from home. You need to have a home computer with a high-speed internet connection and a phone to acquire this job. You also need to have a valid email ID. The work is great for stay-at-home parents, college students, and people who desire a break from their office surroundings.

This is the simplest technique for getting money online. Getting home-based data entry work at a trustworthy firm will enhance your financial picture as well as your career.

Data entry in Richmond, Virginia

D ata entry services are being provided by some companies in Richmond, Virginia. They dedicate their efforts to fulfilling customer satisfaction, and they convert thousands of clients' information into understandable formats. Most companies, big or small, find it difficult to manage the large volumes of complex data, so they need to spend more time and effort handling it.

Companies that deal with data entry in Richmond, Virginia, help those companies by converting their data into usable format, thereby allowing them to spend more time serving their customers to their satisfaction.

Data entry companies take on the burden of preparing, recording, and converting data like invoices, bills, payroll, customer databases, and so on. Since they provide excellent data entry services within the mentioned timeframe, the client companies are relieved of the pressure of data entry processing.

The client companies can trust the firms that work in data entry in Richmond, Virginia, since these companies have safer security measures like monitoring inside and outside of the company with the help of surveillance cameras.

These companies offer 100% customer satisfaction, and they have skilled data entry operators who understand the requirements of client companies and would use the correct tools for troubleshooting. The superior quality of the final output would not compromise timely delivery.

Organizations dealing in data entry in Richmond, Virginia, use the latest technologies. This is important because technical advancements are constantly changing nowadays, so these data entry companies use up-to-date technologies in data entry processing and provide final output accurately. They utilize software and hardware technology for precise data entry.

The data entry companies in Virginia deliver the output in convenient forms like via FTP, email, CD-R, CD-RW, and so on, and they also provide data in various formats like ASCII, fixed length, or comma-delimited as required by the client companies.

They store the data of the client company in a secured place, like a specified warehouse or room with keypad entry. Hence, the client companies need not worry about the security of their data. These companies not only help in data entry processing for client companies but also in the destruction of business documents.

Firms that work in data entry in Richmond, VA, provide valuable services at moderate rates. The pricing would normally vary from company to company depending on the number of keystrokes required to complete the required information. Companies that provide the highest volume of data to process would generally receive some discounts.

Typewritten data is normally charged less than handwritten ones. Similarly, numeric data is charged less than the combination of alpha numeric data. If the client companies require sorting multiple documents, then it would be included in the cost of the project.

These companies deal with the processing of data entry in Richmond, Virginia, for varied projects like credit card applications, surveys, tax information, medical drug studies, data conversion, inventories, insurance, and so on. They can scan documents with the help of a high-speed scanner, which scans lines of data and captures data to a file.

Then they send the file to the client company in the form of FTP or email. They have trained personnel to do the data entry, processing, scanning, etc. accurately.

Data Entry Jobs in Maryland

There are plenty of data entry employment possibilities accessible in Maryland. Those who have the required credentials, like proficiency in Microsoft Excel and Word, along with the capacity to access them online, may apply for the positions. These jobs provide flexible shift possibilities according to your convenience. However, certain organizations may emphasize the first shift, which would help you make more each hour.

Data entry jobs in Maryland give eligible workers several perks that include medical, dental, optical, etc. Skilled workers may earn high rewards for their service in the data entry processing firms in Maryland. These occupations help you enhance your career and financial standing.

There are several degrees of data entry jobs in Maryland. The data entry operator manager is the Level 1 task that demands keying vast volumes of data from source documents into computers for creating entries. The data entry operator managers need to oversee the data entry operator supervisors.

He or she has to have an understanding of the concepts and procedures of supervision. He also has to have an understanding of computer systems connected to data input. He needs to create production plans and make a schedule of work for his subordinates.

Data entry supervisor jobs in Maryland entail planning, organizing, and managing the data entry processing operations of data entry operators. The supervisors need to have an understanding of computer systems and strong communication skills to deal with clients as well as their subordinates.

Data entry operator jobs in Maryland entail executing the responsibilities provided to him or her as per demand. He or she may need to produce data input from paper or books. The data entry operator may also need to make data entry from picture files in the proper format. He or she has to know how to operate the picture scanner for this reason. The image scanner scans every picture file in the source document, and the data entry operator has to change the images into usable format.

There are data entry jobs for home-based individuals offered in Maryland. Since the data entry processing works are getting huge and enormous, the conventional data entry operators alone are not adequate to execute the projects within the required period.

This condition begs for outsourcing data entry tasks to home-based individuals. Any competent individual who has a home computer with a high-speed internet connection may apply for employment at data entry processing firms in Maryland.

Since the data entry sector is continually expanding, data entry jobs may provide stable income. These sorts of employment do not have any pressure, and consequently, many individuals are prepared to join the data input processing firms. As previously said, data entry jobs in Maryland provide a wonderful salary along with other perks. Any individual who has the relevant qualifications may apply for employment.

Data entry jobs in Maryland offer amazing prospects for career seekers. The employment delivers clever cash and permits renewing your career. Since it also provides flexible shift possibilities, you may work at your convenience. You may email you resume via online also.

Demand for Data Entry Jobs

D ata entry jobs are the fastest-growing occupations in the realm of the internet. Every firm, small or large, requires papers typed, such as letters, reports, proposals, manuals, and so on. The corporations find it challenging to handle the vast amount of complicated data. Again, processing data inputs costs additional time and effort, and the organizations find it problematic to concentrate on other concerns.

Hence, data entry tasks are being outsourced to data entry processing businesses. Companies might save time, effort, and thousands of dollars by outsourcing data entry activities.

Data entry processing organizations consequently demand a large number of people, including home-based workers, to complete different sorts of data entry activities. If you have some basic computer skills combined with the capacity to access information online, you may easily make a reasonable income from data entry and processing tasks. Most of the organizations do not demand unique abilities or prior experience for this sort of employment. The ability to follow instructions, albeit not specified by firms, is highly vital for receiving an outstanding salary in a data entry job.

There are numerous sorts of data entry tasks. You may need to fill out the forms in the proper format, or you may need to make data input from paper or books with great speed and precision. The data entry process may also involve producing data from an image file in the desired format. Data input from e-books and business transaction data entry, such as sales, purchases, payrolls, etc., may also be required.

There are certain data entry tasks that may involve producing the final result of data input from hardcopy or printed material in MS Office or any other necessary format. Some firms may require you to conduct strategic data input into a defined software application.

Therefore, a basic understanding of computers like MS Office, MS Excel, and so on is necessary to complete the task. However, it is easy to learn these apps. Even some data entry processing organizations would supply online or face-to-face instruction to you without any fee.

Clerical or administrative data entry jobs are accessible for individuals who have particular abilities or prior expertise in such industries. You may choose home-based data entry tasks too, which gives you flexible alternatives of part-time or full-time. You may complete the task on your own schedule and make smart money.

There are plenty of work prospects for data entry operators. Since the industry is continually developing, you might earn a permanent income from employment. There is no requirement of interacting with consumers, selling things, or other similar unpleasant activities in these forms of occupations. You need to simply perform the work given to you as per the demands of your firm, and you may obtain some reward for your service.

Some sorts of data entry jobs require good grammar understanding and internet and browser usage. Data entry for mailing list and business card data input demands additional attention and care so that you can generate a mistake-free, accurate final output.

There are several businesses that may offer to make you wealthy overnight via data entry employment. It is not true. You cannot get wealthy without any effort.

Like any other job, data entry work also requires specific abilities and effort. However, it may make regular people profit enormously.

How easy is data entry?

D ata entry tasks are made easy today, and thus anyone who has a basic understanding of computers like MS Office and Word and the ability to access the internet may perform this work. It also gives flexible alternatives like day shift, night shift, half-time, full-time, and so forth. Therefore, stay-at-home mothers, retirees, college students, and those who wish to obtain a break from the strain of the office environment may make some excellent cash in data entry jobs.

The rationale behind why data entry is made easier is to give ordinary people a way to make additional work and to be free from the risks of other work. It is a simple means of making money online. The home-based data entry operator might earn equivalent to or more than the standard data entry operator. The ease of working in a home environment without compromising the time necessary to be spent with children is the key benefit of quick data entry jobs.

Data input made it easier for the workers because the organization recruiting them would supply step-by-step instructions that are normally straightforward to follow. Most of the firms would also provide some training to start the job. The staff needs to follow the directions and execute the jobs assigned to them as per demand. These occupations do not require any specific skills or expertise. Thanks to the internet, simple data entry tasks are accessible to everyone dwelling in any area of the globe.

Data input is made simple by certain online firms that ask consumers to perform some typing work in the online form and to submit the forms. But data entry tasks are not identical to conventional typing employment. It demands some talent to disseminate a word on the online forms offered by the firm so that the goods or services of that company will be popularized.

The firms are in significant demand for data entry operators that can operate via the internet and assist in filling out the forms. They are also willing to pay a smart income for the service. People who have the desire to follow the easy directions offered by the organization may acquire these jobs and make some money.

Data input makes it easier to aid those who are ready to work in order to boost their financial picture. In reality, online data entry operators make $20 to $200 per day for straightforward data entry tasks. You need to invest some time according to your convenience and provide an error-free, correct final result to the company employing you.

There are a lot of data entry firms on the internet, and there may be a risk of fraud. However, authentic and reputable data-input-made simple apps are accessible on the net, which you may choose with little effort. You may learn from these programs how to maximize your revenue in the data entry profession.

Therefore, you may email your CV to any of the legal organizations and receive a data entry job, which is easy to complete and will revive your career and financial status.

Outsourcing data entry work

In the quickly growing business world, most firms, big or small, find it challenging to manage the vast amounts of complicated data. They need to invest more time, money, and manpower in data input and processing activities. This issue calls for data input outsourcing.

Outsourcing the data entry work to some other organization will free them from the load of managing data entry activities, and they can invest the time and manpower in some other important tasks like enhancing the quality of products, customer service, and so on. Outsourcing data entry jobs is also cost-efficient.

Data entry outsourcing is the finest alternative for all the company needs that involve expert data entry skills and tools. Data entry processing businesses generally have a huge number of experienced workers who execute any of the data entry processing duties outsourced by the client organization.

They offer the final result as per the necessary format. Since the data entry processing firm itself delivers training and office supplies, the client companies alleviate the worry of teaching the staff and providing equipment to perform the data entry processing jobs.

Data entry outsourcing also allows organizations to have a continuous supply of the final product 24/7, 365 days a year. Hence, firms may outsource any number of jobs and obtain mistake-free, correct output within the set time limit.

Any sort of data entry and processing operation may be outsourced, such as legal documents, manuals, payroll, questionnaires, books, research papers, invoices, tax forms, customer survey forms, medical billing, records, memoranda, financial statements, product registration forms, and much more.

Since the data entry processing firms have security measures like the double-keying procedure, which entails re-keying the data in various files, which are then compared electronically with each other to deliver correct results to the client companies, hiring a reliable organization for data input outsourcing will help the companies obtain respite from most of their data processing concerns.

There are various adaptable data entry processing firms that can support the client company's data input projects, irrespective of the language and kind. In reality, adaptability in handling data entry tasks is one of the key reasons for outsourcing data entry projects. The customer firms may also acquire the result in the desired format, such as via the internet, FTP, CD-R, CD-RW, and so on.

Data entry processing firms offer competent staff that have up-to-date technology in the data entry industry. Therefore, outsourcing the task to them enables you to have the service done using modern technology. These organizations also have high-speed scanners to convert picture files to readable format, and therefore any sort of job may be given to them.

Outsourcing data entry and processing operations to underdeveloped nations is becoming more prevalent today. This helps acquire the necessary outcome for comparably less money. However, cost efficiency does not often indicate the absence of high standards. You will obtain the whole precise data input output at the stated time.

Hence, hiring a competent firm to outsource data entry and processing activities gives a solution to all your information processing demands, so you can concentrate your attention on other business growth operations.

Standards from Data Entry Companies

There are some genuine and reliable data entry processing companies that meet the performance standards required by the client companies that outsource the data entry processing jobs. The diligent and concentrated efforts of data entry companies provide excellent performance to the client companies for comparatively less cost.

Legitimate data entry companies believe in rendering quality services that help increase the performance standards of their clients. For meeting data entry performance standards, the companies require some skills, which include the latest operating systems like Windows 2000 and Windows XP, knowledge of some programming languages so that data entry can be made in the software program or application, knowledge of web design tools, and so on.

The data entry companies also need to have skilled staff that have knowledge of MS applications like MS Office, Word, Excel, MS Access, PowerPoint, and so on. Accounting application knowledge is also essential to meet the data entry performance standards. The staff of the data entry company needs to have good grammar knowledge and excellent communication skills.

Knowledge in some languages other than English may also be required so that the company can be noted for its versatility. The company need not limit its level to some projects alone if it has greater flexibility and adaptability. This would earn a good reputation among the client companies.

The data entry company requires good hardware systems like Pentium and Celeron that have maximum hard disk capability. This helps provide data entry services up to the performance standards required by the clients. Scanners, desk jet printers, CD writers, etc. are essential for the data entry company to provide the final output in the desired form.

The data entry company needs to be available 24/7, 365 days a year. This helps not only to meet data entry performance standards but also helps withstanding in the competitive business world. It should be easy for client companies to contact the data entry processing company.

The data entry company must take safety measures to protect the data provided by the client companies. Using the double-keying process, which involves re-keying the data in different files, which are then compared electronically with each other, can help provide safe and accurate results to the client companies.

Some companies even use powerful cameras to watch inside and outside so that the important legal documents provided by the client companies are safe. These safety measures help meet the performance standards set by the client companies.

Data entry, data processing, and data conversion services should be provided by a data entry company that matches high performance standards in terms of efficiency and accuracy. The company needs to train its personnel to provide error-free, accurate data entry output. Rendering professional-quality services at reasonable costs would increase the data entry performance standards, which in turn would improve the performance standards of client companies.

In fact, the data entry services provided by genuine companies can help improve the rhythm of business activities and thereby increase the profits of the client companies.

They can get relief from the pressure of data entry and processing work and spend that time on other useful tasks like improving the quality of a product or service, increasing turnover, and so on.

Data entry reviews are essential

E ven more so today since there may be more risks of fraud on the internet. You may see various data entry firms that offer to make you wealthy by only filling out the web forms and earning $200 to $300 each day. This was true to some degree before 2 or 3 years. At the early stage of search engines and pay-per-click (PPC) goods, anyone may start working as a home-based data entry operator and fill out the online forms to promote the product or service of any firm.

However, the data input checks done by certain specialists demonstrate that this strategy no longer works currently because the search engines have wised up and efforts have been taken to prevent re-directing websites and false landing pages.

If affiliate marketing does not function, it may not be feasible for a data input operator to make hundreds of dollars every day. However, there are some true affiliate marketing organizations that provide genuine career possibilities for online data input operators. They may generate even a clever income. But remember, there are some dishonest firms that continue to push affiliate marketing that no longer works.

Data entry evaluations assist you in becoming aware of such organizations and preventing fraud. This helps you avoid wasting time and money. Yet there are some legitimate data entry employment chances that enable you to work easily at home and make some additional money.

There are many respectable firms that offer different data entry job possibilities. You may examine this by viewing the data input evaluations regarding such firms. You need to spend little effort to figure out a legitimate data entry employment opportunity. Once you have figured out a legitimate firm, you may next email your resume to that company.

Beware of firms that require upfront payments for training. No excellent firms seek fees for a data input job. However, occasionally, even a respectable organization may impose initial charges to examine the home-based employment chances.

Data entry reviews help you generate money online with the minimum effort. You need to understand the greatest strategies for making smart revenue from data entry jobs. You can also protect yourself from scams.

Some specialists give data-input assessments of excellent firms. You may create them in order to safeguard you from deceptive apps that may make you upset. You need to devote time to studying the reviews before picking a job. This is vital since all the firms would provide a money-back guarantee if it were not feasible to generate a smart income. But some of the unethical organizations would not even respond to your email if you had lost your money by means of first expenses.

Data entry evaluations by specialists give an overall assessment of the firms that help you pick the finest. Also, remember not to trust any business that offers to make you wealthy quickly. No one can gain a lot of money without work.

There may be risks of fraud if a firm says that you may make $200 or $300 by working only half an hour every day. Like any other profession, data entry jobs also involve work and talent.

Data Entry Services

P rovided by several data processing companies, they are essential for any company, whether it is big or small. They help increase your business activities and save you time, money, and effort. Quick and accurate data entry services are provided by the experienced and skilled staff of data entry companies.

The high-quality, cost-effective services provided by data entry companies would help you relieve the pressure of all your information processing needs, and you could focus on other business development processes.

Some of the data entry services provided by data entry processing companies are described below:

1. Data conversion:
Data conversion is an essential service required in this information age. Easy access to data ensures effective business for any type of company. In fact, it saves a lot of time and money. Data entry processing companies help unstructured data be converted into understandable formats using some of the latest technologies. You can get your valuable data stored in paper files or reports converted to digital format so that it will not be lost.

2. Data entry processing services:

Data entry processing services include completing legal documents, manuals, bills, payrolls, questionnaires, tax forms, medical bills, reports, financial statements, and so on. Data entry processing services also include structuring, restructuring, formatting, reformatting, modifying, and indexing data. The data entry processing companies provide accurate data entry services to the client companies.

3. Online data entry services:

Excellent online data entry services are provided by the data entry companies. The services include online data entry, online data entry of e-books, online form processing and submission, online entry from an image file into the desired format, typing a manuscript into MS Word format, online copying, pasting, editing, and indexing data in the required format, strategic online data entry in a software program or application, online data entry from hard copy or printed material, and so on. These companies provide error-free services for online data within the specified time limit.

4. Offline data entry services:

Outsourcing offline data entry to data entry companies is becoming common all over the world. Data collection from various sources, valuable URL list collection, and offline form filling are some of the services rendered by data entry companies.

5. Image processing services:

Data entry companies use high-speed scanners to convert image files into readable formats. They use the latest technologies to provide the final output in assessable form. The skilled personnel of data entry companies offer accurate data entry output through any of the convenient sources, like the internet, email, FTP, CD-R, CD-RW, etc.

The data entry companies offer much more services that can solve your information processing needs. You can outsource either simple data entry work like compilation from e-books, the internet, business cards, and catalogs, or you can outsource converting image files in any format. By outsourcing these tasks, you can enjoy the convenience and security of the work done by data entry companies.

You need not provide training or office equipment to your staff in order to accomplish data entry work. Instead, the data entry company staff, who have experience and skill in doing these tasks, can accomplish the tasks for you. You can therefore concentrate your time, money, and manpower on some business development work.

Testing Your Skills for Data Entry

Data entry skills tests may be conducted by some companies to select the right candidates for the post of data entry operator. Data entry skills tests help filter out the right candidates. The skills test would be conducted with the help of software developed by the company for selecting data entry operators. Normally, the skills tests would be conducted online, and those who passed the skills test would be required to attend an online interview.

Data entry skills tests help in accessing the keyboard skills that include both speed and accuracy. The skills tests would be in various forms, like alpha, numeric, and alphanumeric. You can select any of the forms and attend the test.

Online data entry skills tests are suitable for use in banks, employment agencies, companies, and educational institutions. The unlimited testing features help companies know the skills of their employees or access candidates before employment. The data entry skills test includes the following features:

- ✓ keying modules for alpha, numeric, and alpha numeric tests.
- ✓ Keystrokes per hour and accuracy can be tested.
- ✓ All types of keystroke errors can be logged in the test.
- ✓ Provide a simple way to test the efficiency of the candidates.

The test duration would be 5 or 10 minutes, so the company as well as the candidates need not waste more time.

It is the most cost-effective method of screening the three right candidates.

The skills test is the easiest method of finding eligible data entry operators for both big and small companies. The test would help the company deliver error-free, accurate output to the client companies. It also helps access the work skills of existing online data entry operators.

Data entry skills tests would be conducted with the help of software developed by some other companies. In fact, there are some online tools available that help in assessing the skills of the candidate. They provide various skill-test modules at cheaper rates. The adapting entry companies can make use of such software and conduct the test. The software allows the company to save the test results with a few clicks.

The skills test for the candidates applying for data entry operator jobs is normally a computer-based test. The test requires comprehending and seeing words and numbers on a computer system. The test duration may vary from company to company. But in any situation, it would not be more than 20 minutes. Generally, these tests are being conducted online only. However, some companies may ask that you come in person to attend the test.

If you have any physical disabilities, then separate test accommodations would be provided by the company. However, you need to provide information about the disability prior to the skills test.

The data entry skills test helps evaluate each candidate based on the same set of requirements. It is a fair and systematic way of assessing the candidates. The instructions for the tests would be displayed on the computer screen or online in the case of an online test.

If the candidate has enough practice entering data accurately and quickly, then he or she would be eligible for the post of data entry operator.

Training to Work in Data Entry

Training is offered by the data processing organizations to their staff in order to accomplish the assigned task properly and quickly. The training would be offered either personally or via the internet. the internet. Mostly home-based data entry job training would be supplied via the internet alone.

Anyone who has some basic computer knowledge and the capacity to access the internet is qualified for data entry training. The participants need not have any unique skills or expertise to obtain the instruction. The online training will be offered to all qualifying applicants, irrespective of geography. A valid email ID is nonetheless necessary to access the training.

Some of the data entry tasks, like transcribing jobs, required training. You may need to spend some money to acquire data entry training. You may pay the sum in the form of a money order, a phone order, an order, or a postal check. You may not be able to access the training program until the money has been processed.

You require training for word processing and transcription jobs. The training enables you not only to complete the task properly but also helps you bid a better rate of money for your service. Therefore, you may make a smart income as a data input operator.

You may acquire a home-based data entry job even if you are not a skilled typist. The training program will assist you in obtaining adequate typing abilities that are essential for data entry jobs. The training would also help you pass the data entry skills exam being performed by several firms to identify the proper applicants.

Typing speed and accuracy may be attained through training, and solid expertise in grammar can also be learned through data entry training programs. Typing proficiency and decent grammar are the two essential qualifications for gaining a data entry job.

Transcription data entry tasks like medical transcription or legal transcription need training because the workers need to grasp the medical and legal words in the documents to be transcribed. With transcription data entry training, you may acquire home-based transcription work, as it is one of the leading home-based internet occupations. You are certain to acquire a job with this training, as there is a shortage of people in the sector with suitable expertise.

Another form of data entry work that needs training is data entry research. You need to enter your ideas and evaluations for the research projects in this employment. Training lets you obtain a strong understanding of grammar and typing abilities. Therefore, you may make a smart income with the minimal work of filling out internet forms for research initiatives.

The data entry training length will vary from person to person, dependent on his or her capacity for learning. However, the typical training duration would not be more than a week. Anyhow, the training program is not a waste of money or effort. You will obtain the advantages immediately after getting the instruction.

You would have more possibilities, so you could choose any job you find more suitable. suitable. There are several firms that may provide free training additionally. You may gain such advantages and can start working properly.

Data Entry Jobs Working From Home

A re perfect for all people, and this helps them generate a respectable income. There are plenty of home-based data entry jobs accessible on the internet. The minimal prerequisite to acquiring this job is basic computer knowledge and the capacity to access the Internet. The skill to follow directions when not given by the organization is also vital to executing the task properly and swiftly.

Data input from home employment is more ideal for mothers who need to spend time with their children, elderly people, handicapped people, college students, and those who do not want the strain of office politics. Since these positions do not demand particular skills and expertise, anyone who has minimal educational requirements may apply for them. There is also no age restriction for these occupations.

Data entry work from home demands that you fill out the online forms given by the firm in the proper format. You would need to put your opinion on the form and send it to the firm. The corporations are eager to pay extra for your honest recommendations, as they may help enhance their company.

Most firms are in enormous need of data entry operators like you who can help enhance their goods or services. The firms find it more beneficial to pay you rather than invest in research. Hence, you might get a smart income ranging from $20 to $200 every day.

There are a lot of trustworthy data entry processing firms that might give you real career chances. You may email your CV to such a firm, and you will obtain the job instantly if you have the minimal credentials. Most firms would give online training to their workers, so you could acquire the instruction simply from home.

Data input work from home jobs can offer flexible alternatives like half-time or full-time. This is more useful for parents who wish to spend more time with their children. They may set a comfortable timetable and start working. Since these occupations normally do not have any duties, work-at-home parents may enjoy the stress-free work environment and can make some money to improve their financial status.

Most of the organizations do not demand any prior experience for data entry work from home. However, if you know typing and have a have a solid understanding of grammar, you are certain to obtain the job.

Home-based data entry jobs are a terrific option for regular individuals to make additional cash. However, you need to put in some effort to generate the final product mistake-free and precisely. There may be some unscrupulous firms that claim to make you wealthy through data input and work-from-home employment. This is not, of course, true.

It is not feasible to make thousands of dollars each day in a data entry job. But you may make a high salary in this job. You may renew your profession and financial status without jeopardizing the time you need to devote to your family.

Data Entry

Real data entry jobs require previous experience and/or some typing knowledge. There are a number of scams in online data entry jobs that promise to make you rich over night. It is not true. Like any other job, data entry also requires some modest skills and education. You can earn a decent income in a data entry job by working at home, but it does require work.

You need to spend some hours accomplishing your daily work. The ads saying that half an hour a day is enough to earn a huge income in a data entry job may not be true. Be aware of such scams before planning to send a resume for the data entry job offering those claims.

With the advent of the internet, data entry jobs have been made easy, and a large number of people are working in this field. Clerical or administrative data entry jobs require some basic knowledge, the ability to follow instructions, and the capability to access the internet. Some companies may require previous experience to get the job. Some minimum requirements to get the data entry job are below:

You need to have knowledge of using Windows Explorer, creating folders, copying, moving, deleting, and renaming files.

You may also need to install and run any new software on your computer.

You need to know how to send and receive emails, including on the internet.

You need to know how to use the internet.

In addition to the above, you need to have the ability to accurately and efficiently use the computer to enter data into programs developed for specific projects. You also need to have the capability of following the instructions correctly. Therefore, if you have basic computer knowledge and data entry skills, you are guaranteed to get a suitable job that offers great compensation.

Real data entry jobs offered by reliable companies generally require home-based data entry operators residing in the local area. No employer would like to ship his valuable data source across the country to a stranger to enter the data when he has a number of available typists in the local area.

It is also safe on your part to work for a company in the local area so that you can resolve any queries. However, outsourcing data entry jobs is becoming more common nowadays. Hence, you can select an honest company that offers good compensation for your service, irrespective of the location.

If any company asks you for an initial fee to get a data entry job, say thanks and run a mile in the opposite direction. Generally, legitimate companies would not ask for any fee for a data entry job. You can get a free list of reliable companies offering data entry jobs from some freelance websites, where you can check their ratings and feedback.

The company hiring you for a data entry job would give you either face-to-face training or online training. Then you can start working at your convenience. Most of the companies offer flexible part-time or full-time options.

You can finish the tasks allotted to you without any pressure. You can get payment for your service monthly, once or twice, in the form of a check.

Data Entry Freelance Jobs

Freelance data entry job opportunities are available through the internet. This job helps you maintain flexible and convenient work schedules. It is one of the finest ways to make money online. There is no obligation in a freelance job, so you can enjoy the benefits of working without any pressure.

Since the fast-developing business world has a tremendous work load in field data entry processing, many organizations are becoming more flexible nowadays in order to meet deadlines. They find it impossible to accomplish the data entry jobs with the help of full-time staff alone. Therefore, freelance data entry jobs prove to be the best option for both the companies and the employees who want to get relief from the pressure of the office atmosphere.

If you are an accurate and quick typist, then you can find a genuine freelance data entry job easily and earn some extra cash. You can also enjoy the convenience and freedom of working from home. These jobs do not require any special skills or previous experience. Anyone can do the job if he or she has accurate typing skills. You can also earn some regular income from these jobs since many organizations are in tremendous need of data entry operators, and they are ready to pay you more.

Freelance data entry jobs may be either online or offline. Nowadays, online freelance data entry jobs are becoming more common with the advent of the internet. Some basic knowledge of computers and the ability to access the internet are sufficient for an online data entry operator. He or she need not even have good typing skills.

However, good grammar and spelling knowledge are often desirable. These job opportunities let you earn some extra money without even stepping out of the house. A home computer with an internet connection is enough to earn a living as a freelance data entry operator. There may be a possibility of scams, while some companies offer freelance data entry job opportunities. Some companies may promise to make you rich without any effort. Remember, no one can become rich without any effort. However, freelance jobs for accomplishing data entry work require you to work smart instead of hard.

You need to do some research to find genuine job opportunities. There are some websites that can help you find legitimate companies offering freelance data entry job options. You need to ensure that the freelance job really suits you before selecting a job. You need to select a job according to your capabilities.

Analyze first whether you are capable of writing good articles or opinions in online forms, whether you can type fast, or whether you can do some clerical or administrative data entry work. This would help you select an ideal job and accomplish the work allotted to you accurately.

Freelance data entry job opportunities are available to everyone in the world. A little effort can help you find a legitimate opportunity and earn some extra money. If you deliver the final output as per the requirements without error and within the specified time, you can earn a lot and improve your financial position.

Home Data Entry Clerk Jobs

A home business data entry clerk job lets you work at times convenient for you. It is easy to start a data entry clerk job from home. There are thousands of home-based clerical data entry job opportunities available through the Internet. If you have a home computer with a high-speed connection and a valid email ID, you can start doing a home business data entry clerk job. These jobs are in high demand, so you can earn some extra money as well.

Many organizations find it difficult to handle the large volume of complex data. However, the data entry and processing jobs are indispensable for the smooth running of the business. Instead of hiring employees and providing training and office equipment to them, they find it cost-effective to outsource the clerical data entry jobs to skilled home business owners in the field like you.

The employer, therefore, can save a lot of money and effort. He can spend the time and money saved in clerical data entry jobs on other useful work like improving the quality of the product, increasing turnover, and so on. And on your part, you can earn a regular income by spending some effort and time on these tasks.

In your own home business data entry clerk job, you can develop strong relationships with your clients. If you deliver the final output accurately and error-free, your clients will be satisfied and will give you a larger number of projects.

Unlike a freelance data entry clerk job, here you need to learn some new skills or software so that you can withstand the business world of competition. Developing knowledge of the latest technologies in the field would also help you earn more.

In a home business data entry clerk job, you need to find your own clients. Since you are self-employed, you need to acquire the skills to perform the required jobs, and you also need to maintain office supplies and equipment. However, once you have a good reputation among customers by way of your excellent services, you can earn more money and enjoy a large variety of projects. Most of the companies are ready to pay some great compensation for accomplishing the clerical data entry jobs correctly and promptly.

Your honest approach can bring you a larger number of data entry customers. You also need to remember that you should not limit yourself to some types of clerical data entry jobs. Flexibility and adaptability to varied projects can help you attract more customers and, thereby, more profits.

Starting a home business data entry clerk job is often inexpensive, and it is the perfect solution for many people to earn some extra money from the convenience of home. Though you can set your own timings to work, you need to be careful in delivering the work within the specified time.

If you do not have adequate skills for starting a clerical data entry home business, you can acquire them from some of the online courses. You also need to provide some separate space at home for doing your home business data entry clerk job peacefully.

These simple steps can help you earn a lot.

Data Entry Employment Working From Home

Home data entry employment is perfect for stay-at-home parents, college students, and retirees. You can search for a suitable home-based data entry job from the thousands of job options provided on the net.

Most companies find it impossible to handle a large volume of data processing work. However, data entry and processing are essential for running the business smoothly. Instead of employing staff in data processing work and providing them office supplies and equipment, they find it cost-effective to outsource the work to home-based data entry operators like you.

They are ready to pay great compensation for your service since they can save a lot of time and money they need to spend on data entry and processing.

You can select any type of home data entry employment according to your capabilities. If you are good at writing, you can select articles or opinions in the online forms provided by the company. If you have skills in quick and accurate typing, you can select home-based typist jobs and type documents, manuals, payrolls, tax forms, and so on.

If you have skills in administrative or clerical jobs, then you can select such data entry jobs. There are a wide variety of options, and it is highly up to your own decision to select a job that is perfect for you.

In order to get home data entry employment, you need to have a home computer with an internet connection and a valid email ID. You can select a legitimate company and send your resume. If you have the minimum qualifications required by the company, you would get an immediate appointment.

Most of the companies hiring home data entry operators like you would provide online or face-to-face training in order to do the work accurately. However, you need not pay anything to receive such training. After getting the training, you can immediately start working as per the instructions provided by the company.

Home data entry employment also provides some flexible options like part-time, full-time, day shift, night shift, etc. You can select any of the options according to your convenience. The main advantage of a home-based data entry job is the flexible timing of work schedules.

If you are a stay-at-home parent, a college student, or if you do not want to feel the pressure of office politics, then a home data entry job is the best option for you to earn a smart income.

Since most companies, big or small, are in tremendous need of data entry operators who can help them with information processing work, you can get regular income from this job. If you have enough skill and knowledge in the field, you can then go to the next stage of data entry jobs, like administrative or technical data entry jobs. This helps you rejuvenate your career and financial picture.

Home data entry employment is the best option for companies that want to get relief from an overwork load. At the same time, it also provides benefits to employees who can enjoy the fun of working from home.

Online data entry jobs

Are growing more frequent today. Thanks to the internet, individuals living anywhere on the globe are making a solid income from online data entry and employment. In reality, these tasks are the simplest means of generating money online.

Every firm has to type various papers, such as reports, letters, manuals, newsletters, and so on. Most of the corporations understood that outsourcing the data entry work to other firms was cost-efficient and time-saving. Therefore, online data entry jobs begin to appear all over the globe, and it enables average individuals like you and me to make some additional money.

The simplest type of online data entry job includes filling out forms given by the research business. You need to fill out the online forms and send them to the firm. The corporation, in turn, pays you some money. This job requires no specific skills or prior expertise. All you need to have is decent grammatical knowledge and some basic computer skills. The ability to access the internet is also vital.

There are a number of firms that are willing to pay you extra for the real opinion that you entered in the internet forms. Your comments help them make changes in their goods or services. Since these data entry jobs are more cost-efficient for firms than spending on studies, corporations are prepared to provide high compensation for online data entry operators like you.

There are also some more forms of online data entry jobs. You may need to create data entry from papers or books; you may need to give data entry from picture files in the proper format; or you may need to create data entry from e-books, and so on.

You may acquire some complex online data entry jobs if you have enough experience and competence in the profession. If you offer the final data entry output correctly, then you will be chosen for higher-level tasks, including administrative and technical data entry jobs.

Online data entry jobs demand a home computer with an internet connection and a verified email ID. You may then start working for any genuine company as a data entry operator effortlessly from your house. You may also pick flexible alternatives in these occupations, including part-time, full-time, day shift, and night shift. You may generate some additional revenue without any pressure. It is projected that online data entry operators will earn more than conventional data entry workers.

Online data entry jobs are more ideal for stay-at-home mothers who need to take care of their children. College students, handicapped people, retirees, and those who do not want the strain of office politics may work as online data entry operators, which can stabilize their financial status as well as their careers.

Online data entry career possibilities are accessible to any individual dwelling in any area. The online data input tasks also help firms that may outsource jobs to low-wage nations.

They may have the task done properly by the online data entry operators, and so they can devote their time, manpower, and effort to some other beneficial activities like growing the firm, raising turnover, and so on.

Looking for a part-time data entry job?

Thousands of part-time data entry jobs are available through the internet nowadays. In the fast-developing business world, organizations find it difficult to handle large volumes of complex data, so they are ready to provide flexible options like part-time jobs so that they can run their businesses smoothly.

The employees can also enjoy the benefits of working part-time jobs since they need not compromise the time to be spent with their families.

Part-time data entry jobs are also available for home-based employees. The main qualification required for this job is to have basic computer knowledge and the capability to access the internet. Good grammar and the ability to follow the instructions correctly are also indispensable for home-based data entry operators. They also need to have a home computer with an internet connection and a valid email ID.

Part-time data entry jobs require the employees to do varied jobs like typing forms, letters, and reports or to prepare data entry from pay rolls, records, legal documents, manuals, research papers, tax forms, etc.

The employees need to deliver the final output as per the requirements, and they should also remember to provide the data entry work accurately and error-free. Accurate work would earn them a good name in the company, and they would also earn a decent income from the part-time job.

Part-time data entry jobs are also available for administration and clerical work. Those who have skills in these types of jobs and/or previous experience in the field can get these jobs. Senior employees doing simple part-time data entry work can also get jobs in the administration or clerical fields.

Part-time data entry work is also required in technical fields. The employees need to convert the image files into the required format with the help of a high-speed scanner. Such employees need to have a computer, printer, and scanner at home.

Part-time data entry work is ideal for stay-at-home moms, disabled people, college students, and those who want to earn some extra money other than what they earn from a normal job. Most of the companies would provide flexible part-time options where you could select either a day shift or a night shift. This helps you earn some extra income without sacrificing your family.

Since there are numerous job opportunities in the field of data entry, there may be chances of scams. Hence, you need to put in a little effort to find a legitimate company that offers you a suitable job. You should also remember that part-time data entry jobs also require some skills like good grammar, accurate typing, etc.

Hence, if you want to get a suitable data entry job, you need to develop your grammar, spelling, and keyboarding speed. Then you can get a legitimate part-time data entry job opportunity, and you can earn some money by doing the job in your home atmosphere and at your convenience.

Delivering the accomplished tasks promptly and error-free can help you earn more tasks and, thereby, more money.

Working part-time in data entry

There are thousands of chances accessible on the internet for folks who wish to perform a part-time data entry job. However, you need to make some efforts to find the most suitable one. In the rapidly increasing business world, many companies are becoming more flexible, and they are willing to provide part-time employment opportunities for data entry operators in order to operate their company efficiently. Therefore, part-time data entry jobs are in high demand in all areas of the globe.

Home-based data entry jobs are becoming more prevalent in the sector of secretarial and typing labor. In most situations, home-based data entry operators need to generate reports, postal labels, letters, and other data entry jobs. Most firms, large or small, are in enormous need of information processing labor, so they employ home-based, part-time data entry workers in these activities.

In turn, if they use conventional data entry operators, they need to educate them and supply equipment and other facilities in order to execute data entry processing operations. Hence, the organizations find it advantageous to engage home-based data entry operators to execute these activities. The home-based workers may also enjoy flexible part-time employment and make some reasonable revenue.

A part-time data entry job requires no specific ability or prior experience. The people need to have high typing proficiency and good grammatical knowledge. Basic computer expertise and the capacity to access information online are also required for this work. The home-based data entry operators need to have a computer with an internet connection at home. They need to complete the data entry jobs as per the directions offered by the firm. They are obliged to provide the final result precisely and mistake-free.

Any form of data entry duty may be allotted to part-time workers. The employee may be required to type the papers written in manuscripts, or he or she may be required to type the payrolls, invoices, reports, and so on. Once the part-time data entry operator has enough experience, he or she may be appointed as senior personnel. Then he or she may be offered technical or administrative data entry jobs.

Part-time data entry tasks are great for stay-at-home mothers, handicapped people, college students, and those who wish to make some more money than they get from standard employment. Most of the firms will offer flexible part-time possibilities where you can pick either a day shift or a night shift. This allows individuals to generate smart cash without sacrificing the time they need to spend with the family.

Normally, organizations want to recruit people for part-time data entry if they fulfill fundamental standards like keyboarding speed, accuracy, capacity to follow directions properly, and so on. Hence, if you want to acquire a data entry job, you need to increase your typing speed, grammar, and spelling.

These credentials will give you good part-time employment, and thus you may make a smart income effortlessly at your own pace.

Work at home for data entry companies

I f you are looking for a genuine home-based job, then work-at-home data entry is the best option for you. It requires little effort to make decent money. Data entry is the process of simply filling out online forms and submitting them in the required format. You can understand the work within an hour and start working.

There are some companies that would provide online training to understand the job. Therefore, you need not even step out of your home for the purpose of acquiring training.

The main qualification to get this job is to have basic computer knowledge and the ability to access the internet. You need to have a home computer with an internet connection and a valid email ID.

A work-at-home data entry job is the easiest form of making money online. You can select any of the flexible options, like part-time, full-time, day shift, night shift, etc. You need to accomplish the data entry work as per the instructions provided by the company hiring you.

Therefore, the ability to follow instructions is also essential for doing this job accurately.

Many people earn a decent income from home-based data entry jobs, which you can also do. Most of the companies are in tremendous need of data entry operators who can provide valuable services for them. In fact, the online forms being filled out by you as per the instructions would influence thousands of people, which in turn could popularize the products or services of the company. Hence, they are willing to pay you more for your service.

Work-at-home data entry jobs do not normally require any experience or special skills. However, excellent communication skills and good grammar knowledge may be anticipated by some companies. You need to remember that this job is just more than a normal typing job, and you need to use your ability to fill out the forms in a manner that is influential to internet viewers.

Apart from filling out online forms, you can also get clerical work at home data entry jobs if you have some previous experience in the field. The company hiring you would provide step-by-step instructions, so you would be able to do the job accurately. You can earn $20 to $200 from these jobs.

Since there are numerous data entry companies available on the internet, there may be a chance of scams. You need to do some home work to scrutinize reliable companies. Some dishonest companies may ask you for some initial charges or fees for getting this job. Then beware of such companies since legitimate companies generally do not charge anything for a home-based data entry job.

Once you have selected a legitimate data entry company, you can start doing the simple work and earn a smart income. No matter where you are residing, anyone who resides in any place on the globe can get work-at-home data entry jobs since the work is easy to do without face-to-face contact.

Therefore, you can start a data entry job at your convenience without compromising the time you need to spend with your family.